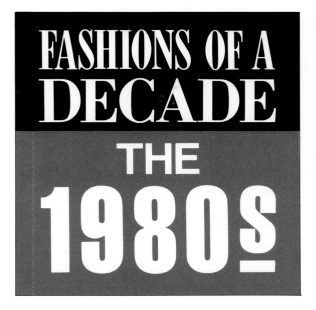

FASHIONS OF A
DECADE
THE
1980s

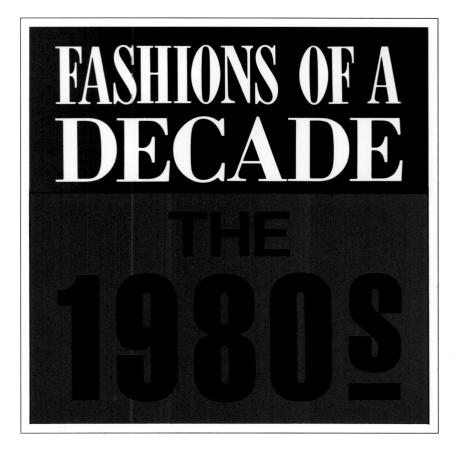

FASHIONS OF A DECADE
THE 1980S

Vicky Carnegy

Series Editors: Valerie Cumming and Elane Feldman
Original Illustrations by Robert Price

Facts On File

Contents

Facts On File, Inc.
132 West 31st Street
New York NY 10001

Facts on File books are available at special discounts when purchased in bulk quantities for businesses, associations, institutions or sales promotions. Please call our Special Sales Department in New York at 212/967-8800 or 800/322-8755.

You can find Facts on File on the World Wide Web at: http://www.factsonfile.com

Text design by Gail Hurstfield
Jacket design by David Stanley
Composition by Latimer Trend & Company Ltd
Printed in Singapore by Kyodo Printing

10 9 8 7

This book is printed on acid-free paper

Library of Congress Cataloging-in-Publication Data
Carnegy, Vicky.
 Fashions of a Decade. The 1980s/Vicky Carnegy.
 p. cm.
 Includes bibliographical references and index.
  Summary: A pictorial survey chronicling the international clothing fashions of the1980s.
  ISBN 0-8160-2471-5
   1. Costume—History—20th century—Juvenile literature.
 [1. Costume—History—20th century.]   I. Title.
 GT596.C33 1990
 391'.009'048—dc20

THE 80s

It had to happen. After the swinging sixties and the excesses of 1970s punk rock, there had to be a backlash. It came in the 1980s, with the art of being serious, grown-up and hard-working carried to the extreme.

But the decade didn't start quite like that. The punk revolution was still in the air – though by 1980, the general trend was to tone down and tame the original punk style. Pop stars such as Prince and Boy George, for example, did not look threatening but rather appealing with their careful makeup and colorful clothes. As the shock effect of outrageous Mohawk hairstyles wore off, even they became simply another form of decoration – just one more fashion. The mood was whimsical and soft, with velvet knickerbockers and short cheerleader skirts. In Britain romance was in the air, with the engagement of Prince Charles and "Lady Di" in September 1980. Their marriage the following July, televised worldwide, fulfilled all expectations. The bride's fairy-tale dress was copied over and over again for less exalted weddings and helped

to set the trend for full-blown romantic evening wear. Were the eighties to be yet another decade of escapist fantasies?

Conventional Prince: Prince Charles and "Lady Di" pose for a formal portrait after announcing their engagement.

Enter the Yuppies

In fact this mood did not last long and the decade soon began to show its true colors. Just as the mini-skirted teenage girl became the symbol of the sixties, so the well-tailored young executive, quickly dubbed a "yuppie," summed up the eighties spirit of hard work and individual responsibility.

This was not just a whim of fashion but a widespread social trend. The election of Ronald Reagan as US president in 1980 ushered in a new decade when it became fashionable to make money and dress well. The Reagans put in motion a fast social whirl, centered around the White House, with smart fund-raising luncheons and evening charity affairs. Just as Ronald Reagan's successful election bid against Jimmy Carter set a new political tone, so Nancy Reagan's designer wardrobe was a total contrast to the informal style of Rosalynn Carter, the former first lady. It was now "in" to celebrate success conspicuously in business or politics with fashionable clothes and accessories. It was not just the West that was encouraging these values. In the USSR, with Mikhail Gorbachev at the helm, some forms of private enterprise began to be promoted and profit was seen as a healthy incentive.

The election of 69-year-old Ronald Reagan was also very much in tune with the demographic changes taking place in North America and Western Europe. Teenagers, if not exactly a dying breed, were dwindling in number as the effects of birth control and marriage at a later age took effect. Youth culture no longer dominated the scene. These changes began to affect fashions as designers and, more important, their financial backers realized money was no longer to be made by aiming for the teenage market. The people they needed to attract were the older professionals who were not only increasing in number but also had the extra income to spend on expensive clothing. Fashion had to become serious

Dressed for success (1): Nancy and Ronald Reagan at their second inauguration ball, January 1985.

The essential accessory for the well-dressed achiever: an immaculate black Porsche.

and recognize that this new breed of consumers did not want gimmicks but clothes that could see them through one business meeting after another.

Reagan and Thatcher – The Conservative Years

Conservative Margaret Thatcher, determined to roll back the post-war socialist era, became the British prime minister in May 1979 and remained in power throughout the 1980s. In the United States her ideological soul-mate, Republican Ronald Reagan, won the presidency in November 1980 and again in 1984. Between them, they set the decade's political agenda. Private enterprise was encouraged and rewarded by favorable taxation. State subsidies, whether to help industry or individuals, were cut – deemed as self-defeating and encouraging people to remain in poverty rather than lift themselves out of it.

Dressed for success (2): How Margaret Thatcher transformed her image: (*left*) in opposition in the seventies; (*right*) in power in the eighties.

Raisa and Mikhail Gorbachev. Like the Reagans, the Gorbachevs looked right in the style-conscious eighties.

Gorbachev

Mikhail Sergeyevitch Gorbachev became the leader of the Soviet Union on March 11, 1985. Aged 54, Gorbachev's relative youth promised change after years of stagnation under Leonid Brezhnev and his short-lived successors, Yuri Andropov and Konstantin Chernenko. But the pace and extent of reform caught the imagination of the world. *Glasnost* (openness) and *perestroika* (restructuring) became part of the international vocabulary as Gorbachev allowed hitherto unthinkable freedom to the Soviet media, began to loosen the state's iron grip on the economy and introduced a measure of democracy. Traditional Marxist-Leninist ideology and history were revised in a way unprecedented since the 1917 revolution. Unfreezing the Cold War in dramatic style, Gorbachev signed a nuclear arms reduction agreement with the US. But at home a reluctant and powerful bureaucracy and continual shortages of basic goods remained a threat to his success.

War and Peace

The decade opened with a rash of bitter regional conflicts. The Soviet occupation of Afghanistan met determined resistance by Islamic Mujahadeen guerrillas. Iran and Iraq embarked on an eight-year war claiming millions of lives. Israel invaded Lebanon in 1982 to root out Palestinian fighters. Most bizarre of all, Britain reclaimed by force the tiny Falkland (or Malvinas) Islands in the South Atlantic after invasion by Argentina. Later, easing of tension between the US and the USSR helped calm a number of conflicts, notably in Southeast Asia and southern Africa. Moscow withdrew from Afghanistan. But civil war still dogged Central America and Lebanon and peace remained as elusive as ever between Israel and its Arab neighbors. Terrorism and civil unrest were never far away in Northern Ireland, where the Irish Republican Army continued to challenge British rule.

Raisa Gorbachev and Nancy Reagan show off contrasting styles of summit dressing diplomacy. By the late eighties power dressing was used and recognized almost everywhere.

Designer Shopping

Calvin Klein, Giorgio Armani and Ralph Lauren targeted their clothes and accessories to this new emerging group, and became three of the most successful fashion emperors of the decade. They spearheaded a "total-look" style of shopping, providing their busy customers with everything they needed, from underwear to overcoats, under one designer label. By the end of the decade, designer-manufacturer Donna Karan was being called "the queen of 7th Avenue" for her toned-down, working women's high-style, yet comfortable, clothing and accessories.

Many large department stores were rearranged to cater to this new way of merchandizing. Inside the stores you no longer looked for the skirt or dress section but went straight to the designer boutique of your choice to add another item to your well-coordinated wardrobe. This at least was the ideal, but many a shopper must have cursed as they made their way from designer boutique to designer boutique in search of a simple item of clothing. Designer accessories, such as Gucci handbags and Rolex watches, became another important status symbol for the "designer shopper."

Chainstores for the younger buyer also adopted this approach. The Italian group Benetton, for example, with franchises in 57 countries, was enormously successful with its instantly recognizable coordinated separates. Even sport and leisure wear came under the influence of designer labels and coordinating shapes and colors. It was not enough to stay in shape – you needed to look good while doing so. On the ski slopes the styles and colors of ski pants changed each season and ski boots themselves became more complex and hi-tech every year. Leotards for workout sessions became high fashion, and trainers had to sport a big name label such as Nike or Reebok to be in fashion. Even the Olympics were almost as much about style

as sport, with the top athletes competing in figure-hugging outfits – not to mention all the razzmatazz of the opening ceremonies.

The 1980s also saw the wearing of trainers move from the playing field, sprint track and health club onto the feet of thousands of working women. Most notably, the widely publicized 1980 New York City transit strike resulted in the popular acceptance of running shoes for the long walk to work. The style quickly gained acceptance and it became commonplace to

see otherwise impeccably groomed working women wearing running shoes for trips to and from their jobs. It was a rare eighties woman (or man) who did not own at least one pair of these comfortable shoes.

Symbol of the eighties – the yuppie woman in her designer suit.

Day and Night – classic eighties couture for day and evening wear, from Claude Montana's autumn 1987 collection. Short skirt, wide shoulders and assertive lines link all these designs.

1988 advertisement for Hennes, a popular chain store in Europe keen to sell the upwardly mobile image of black suit, white blouse, black briefcase – and red Ferrari.

New hair for new dressing: Rei Kawakubo's pastel designs and silver wigs gave a new look to Comme des Garçons' 1989 collection.

The Olympics – opening ceremonies in 1984 (Los Angeles) and 1988 (Seoul). A contrast in Western and Eastern pageantry.

Politics and Sport

Politics dogged the steps of the Olympic movement when the 1980 and 1984 games were marred by superpower squabbling. President Jimmy Carter of the United States tried to organize a full-scale boycott of the 1980 Moscow Olympiad in protest at the Soviet invasion of Afghanistan early that year. In the end, the only significant athletic powers not to turn up were the US, West Germany and Kenya. Four years later, in a tit-for-tat response, the Soviet Union led a boycott of the Los Angeles games by most of the eastern bloc. Superpower friendship ensured a full turnout for the games in Seoul, South Korea, in 1988 – and the games were a great success, despite scandals over the use of drugs by leading athletes.

New Men?

The male image went through some interesting changes in the eighties. The beginning of the decade saw a fantastic peacock look in some quarters, drawing very much on the early nineteenth-century dandy with the use of silks and velvets. An absurdly overblown version was taken up by pop stars such as Boy George, Prince and Michael Jackson, with a lavish use of makeup and wild hairstyles. While women in the 1970s had been fighting to promote a stronger, more powerful image within a male-dominated world, in the early eighties some men seemed to be struggling to create a sympathetic, caring and even beautiful new image for themselves. The rise in popularity of the yuppie look pointed male fashion in a new direction, with more conservatively styled suits and ties becoming high fashion even for youngsters.

New Technological Age

The post-industrial age of computer-based technology became a reality in the 1980s. Perhaps the most dramatic change came in the office with the desktop personal computer, or PC, first pioneered by the American company Apple. It was made possible by condensing large amounts of computing capacity into tiny silicon microchips. Chips were also used to control industrial robots, which increasingly replaced human labour in areas such as car manufacturing. Chips, satellites and other technologies like digital encoding and fiber optics transformed telecommunications, with computer, telephone and television networks spreading all over the world. For the home consumer, new technology meant home computers, video cassette recorders, compact discs and the promise of large-screen High Definition Television.

Wild Prince: Prince in a still from the film *Purple Rain*.

On the surface this looked like a return to the familiar twentieth-century male tradition – but a new spirit was afoot. Care was the key word. Men were increasingly concerned about their appearance and about looking good. Success was not just reflected in salary but in a whole life-style encompassing car, house, clothing and body. Even if you were glued to the computer screen twelve hours at a time, a healthy tan and sleek, conservative appearance were the order of the day. A great interest was taken in the smaller details of clothing and conversations about the finer points of pleats and cuffs were not uncommon.

Even underwear became controversial, with debates over the merits and demerits of boxer shorts, bikini briefs and jockey shorts. Male beauty products finally started to take off as the rugged male image of the seventies gave way to something altogether smoother and more refined. More aftershave, more hair products and even makeup were sold. Even if you couldn't keep up a tan naturally, you could at least fake it and not be ashamed of doing so.

Islam

The power of the Muslim religion burst upon the Western world with the overthrow of the Shah of Iran – a long-standing ally of the United States – in January 1979. He was swept away on a tide of Islamic fundamentalism headed by Ayatollah Ruhollah Khomeini, who, until his death in 1989, symbolized a worldwide resurgence of Islamic consciousness. The intensity of fundamentalist feeling against the West was marked by the holding of US embassy hostages in Tehran for more than a year and, in Lebanon, multiple kidnappings of foreigners and attacks against diplomats and soldiers. Meanwhile, in Iran, Western dress for women was frowned upon: traditional Islamic costume was encouraged as a counter to the influence of the "Great Satan" – the United States.

Dressed for success (3): Michael Jackson on his way to receive a Grammy Award, 1984.

New Women

Just as men were using old female tricks to perk up their appearance so women were at the old game of stealing from the male wardrobe and adapting men's clothing to their needs. This was by no means surprising as more and more women became accepted in high-status jobs. Although the average female earned less than her male counterpart, the female executive was very much a part of the eighties. Her office outfit borrowed from traditional menswear, with various styles of skirt and jacket becoming standard wear. Shoulder pads added width to the female form and lent an air of authority. Perhaps even more than men, women in successful careers had to look good as well as be good at their jobs and exude an aura of success. In the US, 1984 vice-presidential candidate Geraldine Ferraro's style of "power dressing" was a key factor in her political success, while British Prime Minister Margaret Thatcher paid a considerable amount of attention to her appearance – using her manner and dress as one of her tools to win confidence and elections. In a 1985 interview, Thatcher admitted to being a keen reader of *Vogue* magazine. In contrast, the British opposition parties never found anyone, male or female, with a comparable eighties style to challenge her.

East Meets West

The most original ideas of the eighties came from Japanese designers, who showed another way of mixing up the sexes and challenged all the accepted ideas of femininity. The "new" dressing pioneered by Rei Kawakubo of Comme des Garçons and Yohji Yamamoto totally disguised the shape of the body beneath layers of clothing that were often geometric and asymmetric in shape. These clothes rejected traditional Western notions of women's clothes – they were neither obviously feminine nor conventionally decorative. Their unglamorous, functional nature appeared radical to Western eyes, although many of the designs were firmly rooted in Japanese tradition and could almost be seen as a homage to the country's past and a challenge to the increased Western influence there. Men and women were dressed in carefully constructed shapes, echoing kimonos or the simpler shapes of karate jackets.

In the West the new designs struck an immediate chord with the young, who found they had a liking for these stark, severe designs. Black, the color most favored by the Japanese designers, became a widespread uniform for youth. There was an undercurrent of violence in some of the designs, with torn and slashed cloth wrapped around the body – although in a very stylized way, in contrast to the anarchic style of punk. Some saw in this a sidelong comment on a decade when natural and man-made disasters were looked on by some as a portent of the end of the world.

Politics and the Environment

A terrifying explosion at the Chernobyl nuclear reactor near Kiev in the Soviet Union in April 1986 focused the growing concern about man-made threats to the world environment. The Green party in West Germany and groups like Greenpeace and Friends of the Earth had led the way, but now environmental issues were taken up by political parties of all colors. Campaigns highlighted the possible threat of global warming – the Greenhouse Effect – supposedly caused by burning fossil fuels, and the destruction of rain forests; depletion of the protective ozone layer by chemical emissions; and wide-scale industrial pollution. The dilemma, especially for underdeveloped countries, was how to balance environmental protection with economic growth.

Debt and Famine

In the 1970s the West's commercial banks lent huge amounts of money to developing countries. A decade later, unexpectedly high interest rates and economic recession made repayment difficult or impossible for a number of nations. Debt crises in South America and sub-Saharan Africa threatened the stability of the world's banking and financial systems, and the livelihoods of millions in debtor countries were stretched to breaking point by the burden of debt. The biggest sums were owed by Brazil and Mexico, but Africa, owing a total of $200 billion, saw the most desperate results as near-bankrupt nations were simultaneously hit by drought, causing widespread famine and poverty. Western creditors debated solutions, but in the 1980s the net flow of funds continued from poor to rich nations.

Japanese construction. Rei Kawakubo designs for 1981.

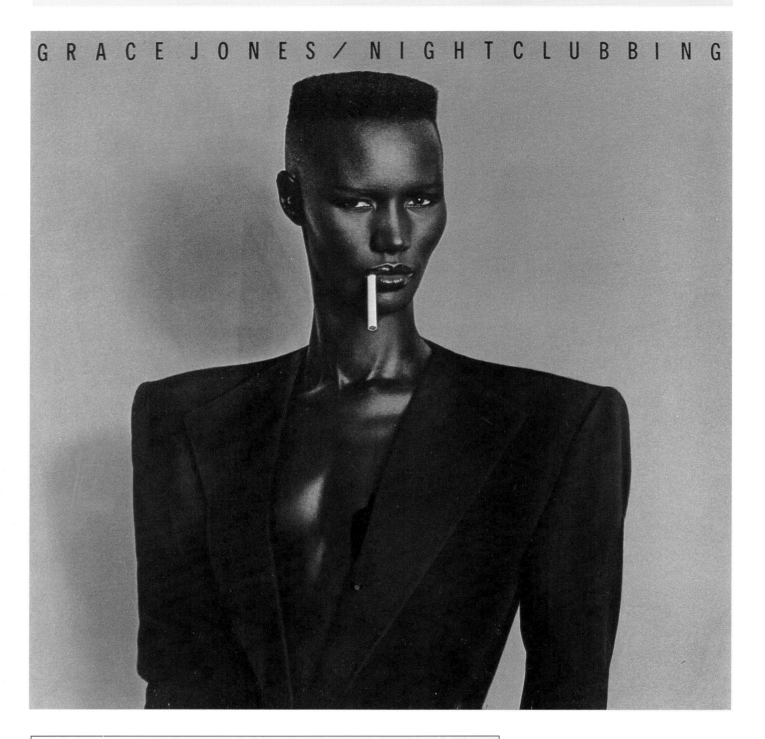

GRACE JONES / NIGHTCLUBBING

Live Aid

July 7, 1985. Probably the most star-studded assembly of rock stars ever play in satellite-linked concerts broadcast on television around the world, in aid of the millions suffering from famine in Ethiopia and other sub-Saharan African nations. The man behind it was unkempt but passionately articulate Irish rock star Bob Geldof. His efforts sparked a tide of similar events throughout the rest of the decade.

"Faces of the eighties": Grace Jones and Annie (Eurythmics) Lennox. Both of these women challenged conventional ideas of feminine dressing.

Into the Nineties

The last years of the eighties saw a relaxation in all areas of fashion. The real peaks of "yuppiness" had passed and a sense of nostalgia for the recent past was setting in. In music the "House" scene emerged in Chicago – dance music that looked back to seventies disco for inspiration and was in sharp contrast to the politically conscious and rhythmically complex rap and hip-hop movements. House soon went worldwide, changing along the way. In Britain, it evolved into the much-touted "Acid House" craze – famous for yellow smiley face badges and notoriously linked with the new synthetic drug Ecstasy. It looked as though a purely fun-loving mood was going to take over.

As so often happens in fashion, the mood of the streets was taken up and transformed by the big-name designers. The '88 and '89 autumn and spring collections were full of fringes, beads and flowers, and the party mood of the revellers was captured in expensive high fashion. Even Rei Kawakubo abandoned the color black, introducing pink rosebuds on shirts for men and pale blue trousers. In exclusive shops expensive jeans with their knees carefully ripped were for sale. Perhaps unsure how to attack the coming decade, some designers were looking back for inspiration and in doing so creating a new fashion mood on which to enter the nineties.

Acquired Immune Deficiency Syndrome

This new fatal illness, transmitted through blood and body fluids, was detected early in the decade in big American cities but appeared to have come from Africa, where its effects were worst felt. Characterized by an inability to resist even minor infections, it was mistakenly labelled an exclusively homosexual problem. Scientists busily researched into AIDS but the public was given little accurate information to help prevent its spread or to allay spiralling rumours and scare stories. By 1985 the World Health Organization reported that AIDS had reached epidemic proportions. Several noted fashion designers died from the disease – including Perry Ellis, Willy Smith and the expatriate American Patrick Kelly. Rock Hudson and Liberace were among those in the public eye to be struck down. At the end of the decade the exact course of the disease was still unknown and no certain cure had been found.

Soul II Soul's rise to stardom popularized the topknot and "funky dread" style of front man DJ Jazzy B.

Pro-Democracy demonstrators occupy Tiananmen Square, Beijing, May 1989.

China

While in the Soviet Union Mikhail Gorbachev was grabbing the headlines for his political reforms, China, the other great communist power of the twentieth century, was undergoing hardly less dramatic economic reform under Deng Xiaoping. Private enterprise and foreign investment were encouraged, leading to a more dynamic economy, although there were problems with inflation. These changes led to growing pressure, especially among students, for greater political freedom. Ironically, a visit by Mr. Gorbachev in 1989 was the focus for huge popular demonstrations, with thousands thronging Tiananmen Square in Beijing. In a bloody reaction that shocked a world watching on TV, the Red Army brutally crushed the protests on June 4. Moderates in government were purged as Deng ruthlessly reasserted the supremacy of the Party.

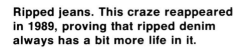

Ripped jeans. This craze reappeared in 1989, proving that ripped denim always has a bit more life in it.

Mini-crinolines hit the runways as part of Vivienne Westwood's 1985 collection.

Romantics, Pirates and Princes

A New Romance

Forget black plastic sacks, safety-pin earrings and rags and tatters, even of the Zandra Rhodes variety. In 1980, most young people had had enough of the revolution and wanted to sink into nostalgia and the cosy comfort of ribbons and bows. The American hostages were still in Iran, the Russians had just invaded Afghanistan, and European unemployment was rising at an alarming rate. Fashion pushed all this to one side and looked back to a different age of silks and velvets, swashbuckling pirates and handsome highwaymen.

Vivienne Westwood, first lady of punk, changed the name of her King's Road shop in London from *Seditionaries* to *World's End* and settled down to producing her New Romantic and Pirate looks, which were greeted with enthusiasm. With leggings and long soft boots falling around the ankles they recalled Errol Flynn movies of the 1930s and 1940s and seemed totally removed from the harsher realities of life.

The pop world caught on to the idea quickly. Prince, in his velvets and laces, actually looked the part his name conjured up. Kid Creole and the Coconuts dressed up as "Tropical Gangsters". Michael Jackson simply went on being himself. Adam and the Ants reflected the mood perfectly with the video of their 1981 hit single "Stand and Deliver." Dressed up as a dashing eighteenth-century highwayman, Adam Ant crashed into a hall of revellers in full romantic dress. Boy George, with his overdone makeup and outrageous costumes, added more fantasy and fun to the scene rather than provoking any challenge to conventional society.

A True Romance

There had to be a fairy tale somewhere to justify all this. The British royal family provided it with the marriage of Prince Charles, the heir to the throne, to the young and charming Lady Diana Spencer. He could not compete with the popstars, but "Lady Di" soon became the darling of the media worldwide. The pageantry of the royal wedding in July 1981 seemed scarcely a part of the twentieth century.

The bride, in her full-skirted dress, designed by the then relatively unknown Emmanuels, fulfilled all romantic expectations. Within hours of its first showing on television it had been copied and placed in the windows of major department stores, ready for other romantic brides to order.

King of the Wild Frontier: Adam Ant poses for the cover of his 1980 hit single "Ant Music."

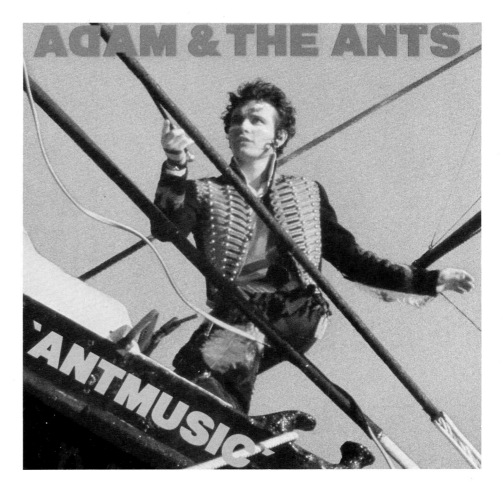

Class Comes Out

The royal romance and the general softer mood of fashion brought into prominence the style of an unlikely set of people. Known as "preppies" in the US and "Sloane Rangers" in the UK, their image was of established and successful families. The clothes they wore were usually timeless classics such as kilts and cashmere twin sets, tweed jackets and cavalry twill trousers.

Robust country wear, such as that provided by L. L. Bean, was important for leisure. Even if you had to stay in the city for the weekend you could still dress as though you were about to go off riding, fishing or hunting. Tradition was fashionable, with a great use of tweed, plaids and intricate hand-knits. Soft mixtures of greens and purples echoed country landscapes and brought a breath of fresh air into the town. The look was too static and staid to remain high fashion for long and a sharper more aggressive silhouette soon emerged.

Prince made sure that the swashbuckling look stayed on the scene right through the decade. This is the cover of his 1986 album *Parade*.

Mini-crinoline craze – Vivienne Westwood's new look for 1985.

Classic country wear: the Burberry.

Fairy tale – the 1981 Royal Wedding.

Hold up stagecoaches in the privacy of your own home: 1980 knickers.

Power Dressing: The City Slicker and the New Woman

Enter the Yuppies

An important new market for designer clothes was tapped in the 1980s: men and women in their twenties and early thirties in high-paying jobs. Hard work was fashionable and a large salary something to be shown off in expensive cars and designer clothes. European companies were increasingly abandoning their more traditional approach to recruitment and adopting the American practice of rewarding young talents fast with good jobs and good salaries. The term "yuppie," standing for "young upwardly mobile professional," was coined to describe the phenomenon. While few would admit to being one, the "yuppie" market became an important target for advertisers selling everything from cars to instant coffee through portraying a wealthy, successful, hard-working but young life-style.

The Aggressive Silhouette

The look produced by the designers in the early 1980s for this market was, essentially, based on the male silhouette. Wide shoulders were the key, emphasized with pads. For the day, the suit was essential for both the working man and woman. His was, typically, double-breasted with front-pleated trousers, creating a broad, powerful image. For her the jacket was worn over a safe on or below-the-knee-length narrow skirt. The classic Armani jacket, hanging loosely from wide shoulders, disguised the waist and narrowed the hips, leaving hair, makeup and legs to proclaim femininity. In contrast to the aggressive exterior, underneath

Bodybuilding – for both sexes – was an eighties craze. Bodybuilders shared many goals with power dressers – the desire to be noticed, and to appear commanding and confident in all situations.

32

many women began to wear frilly feminine underwear, and companies such as Victoria's Secret capitalized on the market for these garments. Glamor was kept for evenings. The increasing popularity of formal events such as charity balls was an opportunity for female display, while men were provided with a ready uniform in the dinner jacket or tuxedo.

Beneath the clothes the body too was being molded into a powerful form. Exercise was important in the 1970s but concentrated on slimming down the figure. In the early 1980s body building and exercise machines became the fashionable way to stay in shape. The aim, for women as well as for men, was to attain a strong, powerful figure. The most extreme profes-

Television helped spread the power dressing message. Characters in "Dallas," "Dynasty" and "LA Law" dressed to impress – and the public followed suit.

Geraldine Ferraro on the campaign trail – power dressing at work.

sional female bodybuilders upset all conventional ideas of the female form, echoing the rejection of the traditional feminine role by the successful businesswomen. In 1983 Calvin Klein summed up this mood, perhaps lightheartedly, with his jockey shorts for women. They proved to be a best-seller.

Designer Life-style

Calvin Klein and Ralph Lauren in New York and Giorgio Armani in Milan worked this "yuppie" market to the hilt. They realized the importance of creating and controlling the right image for their clothes through their own advertising, rather than leaving it to fashion editors to bring them to the buyers' notice. They could provide a total look not to be mixed with anyone else's designs. They lived the lifestyle they designed for, being as much astute and successful businessmen as

Sylvester Stallone – but are those shoulders really all his?

creative designers. The importance of hitting the right image was shown by the success of the German designer Hugo Boss. His sales soared by 21 percent when his suits were worn by television actors starring in "Miami Vice" and "LA Law." Suddenly he was selling not just a beautifully tailored suit but an exciting and successful image.

Boom or Bust?

For a short while after the 1987 stock market crash it seemed as if the yuppie look and life-style were going into retreat. But this never quite happened. The aggressive fashionable look certainly softened, with shoulder pads for women becoming less important and men's suits slimmer in line. But the overall look remained important throughout the eighties, with the business suit for men and women an important fashion item. The designer empires built up on this market continued to flourish and looked set to expand in the 1990s.

Princess Diana began the eighties as a fairy-tale bride (see page 31), but ended them dressed as a chic go-getter.

The preferred working uniform of the eighties male. Double-breasted, square-cut tailoring suggests substance, strength – and money.

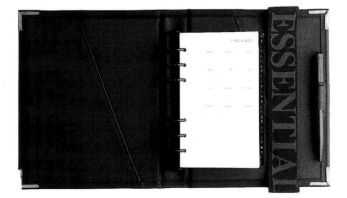

Work never stops, and time is money. A personal organizer and cellular phone became *the* symbols of the urban professional's way of life.

This 1988 evening dress by Enrico Coveri combines sumptuous glamor with an aggressive, wide-shouldered silhouette.

Cut, Shape and Drape

Invasion from the East

In 1981 the Japanese really came to town. Rei Kawakubo of Comme des Garçons presented her collection in Paris. Not yet part of the accepted fashion scene, she showed her clothes on hangers at the Hotel Intercontinental in Paris and the fashion editors flocked to see them. Soon Yohji Yamamoto opened a boutique in Les Halles, Paris. Already well established in Japan they now set out to conquer the West with their own unusual style.

Not everyone was enthusiastic. The prestigious *Women's Wear Daily* labeled their image "the Hiroshima bag lady look." Others were completely won over by a style that ran against all the current high fashion rules. Their clothes seemed to start from a totally different basis from the traditional Western designers. Instead of using the body as the basic form, these garments could completely disguise the person beneath and were sometimes more like sculpture in their exaggerated shapes and textures. They also acted as a reminder that fashion developed very differently in other parts of the world.

Kawakubo's work in particular, although stylized as part of the "new" dressing and claiming to be influenced by nothing from the past, did echo traditional Japanese motifs.

Yohji Yamamoto and models with his spring 1986 collection.

A Look to Live in ...

Both Kawakubo and Yamamoto claimed to be making functional clothing for working people rather than for the super rich and leisured. Certainly their unusual shapes and heavy use of black were popular with the young. "There is nothing so boring as a neat and tidy look" was printed on the labels of Yamamoto's inexpensive range, an idea almost bound to appeal. In fact their garments required a good deal of dedication to wear and could even be physically difficult to get in and out of. The look was meant to be total and never to be mixed up with other designers' work. They were sold only in carefully controlled retail shops that could guarantee to carry a full range of the designs. Both designers were known for the attention

Less is more: a Comme des Garçons retail outlet.

they paid to the architectural detail of their own boutiques. In total contrast to the complex garments, often multi-layered and heavily textured, these were sparse and minimalist.

Reply from the West

It took three years for any Western designer to come up with such a new and challenging look. Then, in 1984, Romeo Gigli in Milan suddenly produced his softly draped "Italian Madonnas," which, again, were a total contrast to all the current looks.

In London the young fashion student John Galliano became instantly famous for his "Les Incroyables" collection. Gigli and Galliano used ideas from the past to create a new and challenging image, although one more easily understood by Western eyes. The high-waisted silhouette did not disguise the body underneath, revealing instead its natural contours. Set against the very powerful, formal image of the city slicker this was as much of a shock as the asymmetrical layers of Yamamoto.

Texture, muted color, unusual cutting: Comme des Garçons separates for Spring 1987.

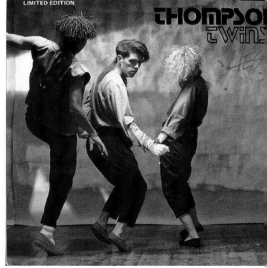

Breakout: the Thompson Twins made it big in 1983 and took on board the new image from Japan.

Issey Miyake took cutting and shaping to further extremes than anyone else, disguising and even hiding the body beneath.

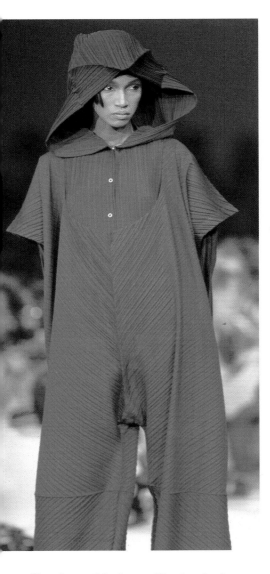

Shaping – this Issey Miyake design for 1989 successfully confuses our normal ideas about shape and proportion.

Romeo Gigli provides an interpretation of cut and shape, which is, in its own way, as unexpected as the designs from Japan.

Bizarre and Absurd

The Wild Side

Why do we do it? Fashion is mad. Few of the clothes we pull on every day are made just to keep us warm or cool or dry or even comfortable. Even fewer of the clothes in the glossy magazines have anything to do with these qualities. We squeeze ourselves into shapes, change from short skirts to long, or from tight jeans to baggy pants and then, in a matter of months, are ready to move on to something new yet again.

The clothes shown on the catwalks by major designers reflect this urge for change and help to fuel it. Some of the wildest ideas may never be worn in the street but they stimulate thought and act as a challenge. In the 1980s Jean Paul Gaultier showed a range of men's skirts. If women can wear trousers what is so odd about men in skirts? Christian Lacroix deliberately set out to amuse and intrigue with his fantasy shapes and rich decoration. Vivienne Westwood attacked the wide-shouldered, slim-hipped silhouette of the 1980s female executive with her "mini-crinolines," which influenced countless party dresses, even if her original design remained too bold and strong for the mass market.

Escape!

Was reality just too hard to take? Throughout the decade flights to fantasy land were always available. Space and adventure films were wildly popular and provided an easy way of forgetting about life's problems. In the pop world two megastars, Michael Jackson and Madonna,

fueled their success by making their public image more weird and wonderful each month. Madonna's look-alike fan club had a hard task keeping up with each change.

The more adventurous were not satisfied by mere copying. There was a strong nightclub scene for those who wanted to create their own fantasy. To get into the best it was not enough to have money — you had to have "style," and the right style for each changing week. Clubs were notorious for a while, then abandoned by anyone at all in the know.

The nightclub scene was brought onto the runways by designers such as Patricia Field, John Galliano and the Body Map team. Sometimes adored by the fashion press, at other times detested for their weird amateurish approach, at least they could be relied upon to be different. The shows were often more like theater, presented with long and sometimes incomprehensible titles and including friends and followers as well as professional models.

Material girl. Madonna's stage gear took some of the street fashions of the early eighties to the limit.

Gaultier's skirts for men — one idea that didn't catch on.

Secret Outlets

For the more timid there was an easier way to add just a hint of the fantastic to their lives. There was an explosion of small accessories covered with exotic and ridiculous motifs. Socks and underpants were the two main targets to be covered by all sorts of patterns from black-and-white keyboards to Mickey Mouse. The success of the 1989 film *Batman* led to a period of total Batmania, with bats printed on everything from boxer shorts to toddlers' sweatshirts.

They only come out at night: clubbing at New York's Palladium.

Bizarre: Karl Lagerfeld is fond of introducing everyday shapes and objects into his designs, often creating a surreal effect. One design from 1983 featured a shower that sent glittering "spray" down the model's back.

Unusual combinations of leather and wool, color and cut in this 1988 mini by Christian Lacroix.

Michael Jackson, always one step ahead of the game.

Hip-Hop, House and After

Get Up Offa That Thing

By 1981 the trend was clear – the eighties were set to be the decade of dance music. The "discos" of the seventies re-emerged as *the* places where street sounds and street fashions were made. New York clubs led the way, with DJs such as Larry Levan of the Paradise Garage and "Jellybean" Benitez of the Funhouse mixing the sounds and getting involved in the production side as well – Madonna was one of Benitez's early discoveries. But most of the new dance-floor stars were black artists: Afrikaa Bambaata, Grandmaster Flash and the Furious Five, Planet Patrol, Run DMC. Meanwhile, soul music's established dance-floor fillers – James Brown, Hamilton Bohannon – gained a new lease on life, while jazz superstar Herbie Hancock re-emerged as king of the dance-floor with the smash-hit "Rockit."

Serious dancing meant a serious dance style – clothes that were eye-catching but also comfortable to move in. In 1982–83 the look might be short black studded leather jackets or denims mixed with "spray-on" trousers for the girls; cut-off shorts, baggy drawstring shorts (or shorts on hot nights) for the boys. Athletes' sweatbands at the wrists marked the really devoted dancers; sneakers or similar footwear were a must.

Afrikaa Bambaata and Soulsonic Force – breakdancing black superheroes.

Bodypopping

The electrobeat sound had taken over the dance floors by 1984 – records built around a drum machine and synthesizer sound, the words usually rapped instead of sung. Breakdancing had emerged as an international craze – falling on your back ("body slam"), spinning on your back ("helicopter"), even spinning on one hand ("one hand glide"). Breakdancers formed teams or "crews," held street shows, competed in championships – national and international. But you had to be young and very fit.

The look was minimalist. Sportswear became a necessity: nothing else could stand up to the wear-and-tear of bodypopping. Labels became "crucial" – Adidas, Nike, Reebok sneakers. Knowing which were the labels to be seen in meant being part of the scene yourself: anything that made it into the magazines was already out of date.

House and After

The edgy sound and jerky dancing of the Hip-Hop movement had a street-wise, even aggressive, feel. They reflected the pressures of inner-city life. By the mid-eighties, a new black sound had emerged from Chicago – the House movement. House music drew its inspiration from seventies disco, jazz or Latin music. Artists and fans preferred to dress up smart – big jackets, "Miami Vice" style suits. By 1988, House had diversified and was no longer just an American movement. The stylized "Vogue-ing" became popular – a dance which resembled watching a freeze-frame movie. Italy was fast becoming an important center of record production, while in Britain media attention focused on the Acid House craze: famed as much for the packed, semi-legal warehouse parties and eye-catching fashions as the music itself.

Acid House looked back to the sixties for many of its ideas – brightly colored or fluorescent tops, worn outside loose denims, pedal-pushers or harem pants in bright "acid" colors. Tie-die and batik or African-inspired prints mixed in with lycra cycling shorts and other familiar items from the sportswear shops.

Neneh Cherry, daughter of famous jazz trumpeter Don Cherry, made it big on her own account in 1989. Glamorous and sophisticated, her image is still very much about moving and dancing with freedom.

The Face, 1984. Spreading the dance word on both sides of the Atlantic.

Crossover

Most of these fashions only reached the suburbs and the chain stores in a watered-down form. But – like the new shapes of Kawakubo and the other Japanese designers – they made their presence felt in unexpected ways. The eighties obsession with dance and exercise ensured there was always a big following for the latest dance sounds – even of the less safe and familiar variety.

Black designers were gaining attention for their clothes through the popularity of the music that went with them. By the end of the decade, House and Hip-Hop had become the single biggest influence on youthful street fashion, while a new generation of recording stars – Adeva, Neneh Cherry, Soul II Soul – looked set to carry their influence into the nineties.

45

PUBLIC ENEMY

Public Enemy – increasingly, the public face of Hip-Hop, especially after they recorded a track for Spike Lee's 1989 movie *Do the Right Thing*.

Breakdancing. Sportswear was the only option if you wanted to spin on your head in 1983.

Dancing in the street. Details and labels may go in and out of fashion, but stylish freedom of movement remains the key.

Bodypopping at The Funhouse.

Second Skin: Design in New Fabrics

Workout!

In the 1980s you had to be fit. Not just thin but *fit*. Whether you were Madonna or the president some form of exercise was obligatory, and exercise that hurt and worked those muscles. Aerobic and dance studios, gyms and weight machines sprung up like mushrooms. Exercise books, cassettes and videotapes sold by the thousands for those too shy to work out in public. Muscles had to be toned, fat worked away and the body firmed up like an Olympic athlete's. If you dropped out of your class at least you could live your fantasies at the movies with films like *Dirty Dancing* becoming big box office hits.

In Love with Lycra

Once you had the shape, you needed the right clothes to show it off. Suddenly even brief running shorts looked old hat and baggy. Figure-hugging Lycra looked good and was better aerodynamically too. Florence Griffith-Joyner, better known as Flo-Jo, stunned the world not just with her record-breaking running but with her skintight, brightly-colored, one-legged outfits. Lycra shorts became high fashion. So did bicycling, as long as you were a city messenger weaving your way in and out of heavy traffic on an unwieldy mountain bike. Lycra leotards in neon colors were worn not only in the exercise studio but to parties too, with a figure-hugging skirt as cover-up. With Lycra tights coming on to the market you could be encased in this wonder fabric from top to toe. Very decently covered, but with every curve and ripple of well-worked muscle outlined.

After Lycra it was a simple step to move on to rubber. Latex, a form of rubber that lets air through, was used first for water sports and swimwear and then for clinging tops, skirts and shorts. You had to be brave to wear it, and to have worked hard at all those classes.

Flo-Jo. The Olympic Gold Medal sprinter Florence Griffith-Joyner became as famous for her stunning fashion sense as for her record-breaking running at the 1988 Seoul Olympics in Korea.

Design-a-Body

For those who wanted the shape but didn't want to look as though they had come straight from the sports field or out of the pool there was only one top designer. Azzedine Alaia became a fad in the eighties, although he had been dressing famous women from his studio in Paris for the last thirty years. His artfully constructed dresses of leather and clinging fabrics showed women off to their best advantage, concealing flaws as often as they revealed alluring curves. He combined the flair of street style with the assurance of high fashion to create a powerful look that was very much of the decade. In other hands the same materials looked tacky. An exercise for the catwalk rather than to be worn in real life.

Underpinnings

Taut and toned as it was, this ideal body did not need any serious support in the form of wired bras or girdles. It became rather difficult to sort out what was underwear and what should go on top – as sporty looking shapes were sold as bras and tight leggings worn as trousers. It was the shape underneath that counted, and if you didn't have it you were better to leave Lycra and Latex alone.

A unisex look is the message of this high-fashion Lycra cyclewear.

Rubber Soul. These Neils Jorgensen designs make use of the cutting and draping possibilities of rubber, as well as its more obvious stretching and clinging qualities.

Work that body! Lycra exercise wear plus an important exercise accessory – the bike.

These influential Azzedine Alaia designs were first seen in 1987.

A new shape for the late-eighties mini – wool jersey combined with Latex for the Aquagirl look. Argentinian/ Australian designer Willy de la Vega also produced a popular range of Latex swimwear.

Retro Fever

Retreat to the Past

If keeping up with the fast-moving eighties became too hard, the safest thing to do was to sink into an older and better world. The only problem was that the past was moving fast too. If you hadn't changed your wardrobe for ten years it was more than likely that you would become highly fashionable again.

Fashion nostalgia was certainly nothing new, but in the eighties it was taken to extremes, with the very recent past being plundered for ideas. The fifties, the swinging sixties, even punk were all recreated, with a little something of the present being added as well. It might be just in slight touches, such as a pair of sixties-style ski-pants, or a bizarre total imitation of punk style only a few years after the whole thing had died.

Even the most forward-looking designers were looking to the past by the end of the decade. Yohji Yamamoto's 1989 autumn menswear collection paid homage to the America of the 1950s, with sweaters and zipper jackets inspired by the baseball field, while Yves St Laurent was reviving flower power with loose floral shirts for evening wear. Odd reminders of the past could turn up when least expected, such as Jean Paul Gaultier's use of thick-soled Doctor Marten boots. Advertisers quickly latched on to the retro bandwagon, using the music and images from previous decades to sell goods to the fashion-conscious youngsters of this one.

Rock 'n' Roll Goes On

The continuing popularity of the sounds of the sixties and seventies kept the fashions of those decades alive as well. There was always a hard core of people who remained attached not only to the music of their youth but also to the natural, informal look they had adopted as rebellious teenagers. But there were also 1980s youngsters who fell for the long hair and ragged, faded jeans look, as well as the music that went with it.

Throughout the 1980s the sounds of previous decades kept popping up in the charts. In 1989 Bob Dylan, The Rolling Stones, The Who, The Beach Boys and Paul McCartney were all touring and releasing new albums. As though in sympathy fashion saw a brief revival of ethnic-print skirts, deliberately ripped jeans, fringing and beads recalling the era of the Woodstock pop festival twenty years earlier.

Image from the past: the Stray Cats, Los Lobos, Kid Creole and the Coconuts, The B52s and Elvis Costello making use of "retro" images on record jackets. A whole book could be filled with similar examples.

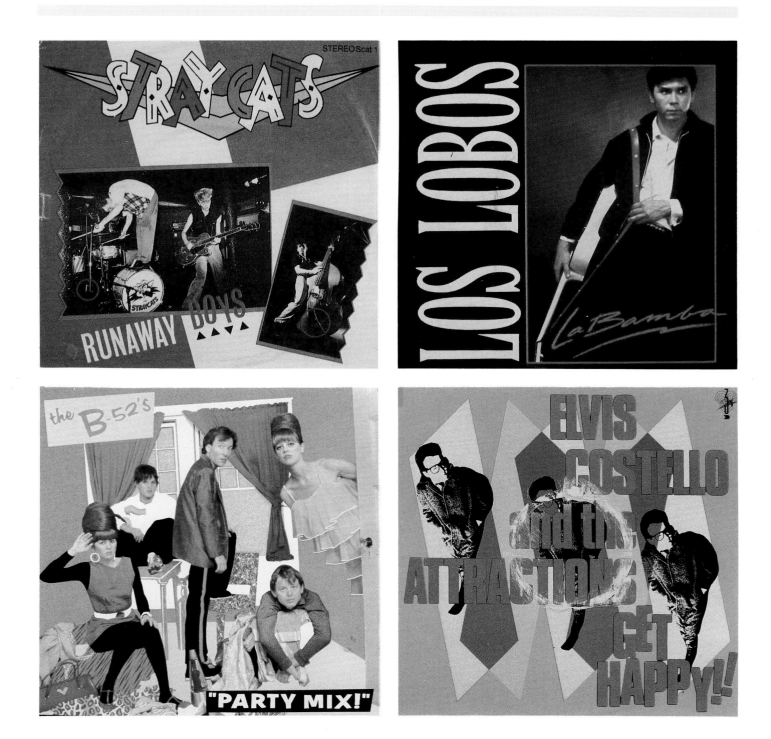

Secondhand Chic

For some people looking back to the past was a dedicated quest for quality, style and cut, which they felt contemporary clothes could not provide. Thrift shops, charity shops and garage sales were all raided for additions to the wardrobe and also the home.

Anything from horn-rimmed sunglasses to a double-breasted suit of forty years ago could be tracked down and picked up for considerably less money than the latest fashions being sold in the chic department stores. A complete look from a chosen decade could be painstakingly reconstructed in original clothing, but most people looked to the thrift shops to find something cheap and individual that could add just that fashionable touch of the past to their modern wardrobe.

Another "retro" denim design from 1989 – this one by Katherine Hamnett.

This Giorgio Armani evening dress looks back to the late sixties for its inspiration. The styling and pose of the model artfully add to the effect.

By the end of the decade, the rural past was once again providing inspiration to city-dwelling designers and customers – whether your preference was for Ralph Lauren or Laura Ashley.

Looking Forward – Into the Nineties

Prime Time

Age looks set to become a dominant factor in the fashions of the nineties. The populations of North America and Europe are changing, with many more people in the 45–66 bracket and fewer 16–24-year-olds. The traditional youth market may become less important. Fashions will have to adapt to dressing the *woopie* – the "well-off older person" who will have the money and leisure to spend on expensive clothes and accessories.

Barbara Bush has already set the tone. As first lady, Nancy Reagan was always fashionable but her wardrobe and pencil slim figure were modeled on clothes designed for women many years her junior. Barbara Bush's style is elegant but matronly. She has proved that you can still look good without pretending to be young. American designers such as Donna Karan and Calvin Klein are already in the lead in providing toned-down grown-up fashions for an older market, both for leisure and work. European designers, with their greater emphasis on innovation, are lagging behind.

Global Environment

The world also seems to be growing more fragile. The late eighties saw a growing awareness of the damage being done to the environment and it became more fashionable to be "green" and environmentally aware. This had the greatest impact on beauty products with "ozone-friendly" hairsprays, non-animal tested cosmetics and fruit-and-flower based oil and scents becoming not just a fashion craze but a social duty.

Shrinking World

Ever-improving communications are making the world seem yet smaller. Popular American TV series are shown on television in countries all over the world, bringing a knowledge of Western fashions to remote rural areas. But the fashion traffic is by no means one-way, with shapes, colors and textile designs continually being imported into the West from other countries as travel becomes easier and quicker. The traditional fashion centers of Paris, Rome, New York and London have already had to face up to challenges from Japan and Germany. In the nineties it looks as though countries such as Spain, Portugal, Australia and even Turkey will be coming to the fore.

Good worldwide communications make the pirating of designs even easier, as pictures can be sent from one country to another at the touch of a button. Cheap copies of new ideas can be manufactured and in the clothing stores in a matter of weeks. The nineties look set to change fashions at a frantic pace.

Fashion for others. Fashion jumped on the Band Aid bandwagon in 1986. Grace Jones, Marie Helvin and Jerry Hall get ready for the show.

Back in the USSR. East meets West in these streetwise fashions from Gorbachev's Soviet Union. For evening wear, a more traditionally Russian look is favored.

Formal. Black or white, East or West, dapper was still the way to be as the eighties turned into the nineties.

Setting the pace. Informality isn't just for the young. In fact, fashion has come full circle, and the affluent older consumer has become as important as the teenage fashion market became in the sixties.

Two-way traffic. King Sunny Ade and his African Beats mix Western and West African styles on a 1983 record jacket.

Dressed for success (4): Barbara Bush brought a new and more relaxed style to the White House in 1989.

Glossary

Alaia, Azzedine (dates unknown) French designer, born in Tunisia. Worked for Dior, Mugler and others before forming his own label in 1982. Famed for his figure-hugging dresses in leather, cashmere and stretch fabrics.

Aquagirl Swiss-based label formed by Argentinian/Australian designer Willy de la Vega in 1986, originally specializing in Lycra and Latex designs for sports and beach wear.

Armani, Giorgio (b. 1935) Italian designer. Formed his own label in 1975. Famous for his suits and jackets, especially the wide-shouldered look for executive women.

Benetton North Italian family firm established in the early sixties by Luciano Benetton. Benetton remained popular throughout the eighties for their colorful casual wear and knitwear separates.

Body Map British design partnership formed in 1982 by David Holal and Stevie Stewart.

Burberry Company founded by Thomas Burberry (1835-1926) in Dorking, England, manufacturing gabardine rain and sportswear. The company continues to flourish and set standards in this field.

Boss, Hugo (dates unknown) German menswear designer who achieved prominence when his suits were worn by characters in "Dallas" and "LA Law".

Coveri, Enrico (b. 1952) Italian designer. Established his own label in 1979. Coveri is famous for his youthful, fun-loving designs.

Comme des Garçons Label formed in 1969 by Rei Kawakubo (b. 1942). Kawakubo's designs attract attention by their muted colors and radical approach to cutting and shaping.

Couture An abbreviation of the French phrase *haute couture*. Haute couture has in the past meant individually created garments, but in recent years the expression has also been used to refer to limited editions of designer garments.

Doc[tor] Martens Hard-wearing British workingmen's footwear, fashionable with young people in Britain during the eighties.

Emanuel, David and Elizabeth (both b. 1953) British designers, born in Glamorgan, Wales. They shot to prominence as designers of Lady Diana Spencer's dress for the 1981 royal wedding.

Hamnett, Katherine (b. 1948) British designer who established her own business in 1979, becoming particularly successful in the Italian and British markets. Her large-slogan t-shirts of 1984 created considerable impact.

Galliano, John (dates unknown) British designer, who broke through to instant fame with his "Les Incroyables" collection of 1984. Innovative and even quirky, Galliano is very popular with the younger buyer.

Gaultier, Jean Paul (b. 1952) French designer, who started his own company in 1977. He is now one of the most influential of the French ready-to-wear designers, whose work continued to surprise and provoke throughout the eighties.

Gigli, Romeo (dates unknown) Italian designer, who worked for the Callaghan label before forming his own company in 1983. 1984 brought him widespread acclaim with his "Italian Madonna" look.

Hennes Inexpensive Swedish fashion chain, very active in the younger market in Europe in the late eighties.

Kamali, Norma (b. 1945) US designer, based in New York. Kamali formed her own label in 1978, and received widespread acclaim throughout the eighties for her fashionable sportswear and office wear for the executive woman. She has also been innovative in her approach to fabrics.

Karan, Donna (b. 1948) US designer, who worked for Anne Klein until forming her own label in 1984. Renowned for her wearable sportswear and stylish clothes for the mature woman.

Kenzo (b. 1940) Japanese designer, working under his own Jap label in Paris from 1970. A successful blender of Eastern and Western styles, Kenzo paved the way for the wider popularity of Japanese designers in the seventies and eighties.

Klein, Calvin (b. 1942) US designer who started his own business in 1968, initially specializing in suits and coats. His smooth, understated look has been a key influence in the eighties, especially in the USA.

Lagerfeld, Karl (b. 1938) German designer, based in Paris, who worked for Chloe, Krizia and Chanel before launching his own collection in 1984. His imaginative and witty designs remained a major fashion force throughout the 1980s.

Lauren, Ralph (b. 1939) US designer, who worked for several menswear clients before launching his own women's label in 1972. 1978 saw the launch of his influential "prairie look," featuring denim skirts worn over layered white petticoats. In the eighties, Lauren upheld the tradition of quality fabrics for menswear and womenswear, and became something of a cult designer for the Yuppie buyer.

Miyake, Issey (b. 1935) Japanese designer, born in Hiroshima. Worked in Paris from 1965 and with Geoffrey Beene in New York from 1969, before forming his own label in 1971. Miyake was extremely influential in the 1980s with his bold cutting and draping, and his innovative use of textures and sculptural shapes.

Montana, Claude (b. 1949) French designer, who worked in jewelry and leather before launching a collection of clothing under his own name in 1977. He shows great flair with sportswear as well as leather, and remained a consistently influential designer in the eighties.

Mugler, Thierry (b. 1948) Designing under his own name from 1973, French designer Mugler has been a leading exponent of the "hour-glass" and figure-hugging fashions of the 1980s, although the styles of his clothes are often influenced by fashions of the forties and fifties.

Westwood, Vivienne (b. 1941) British designer, closely associated with the rise of the punk movement in the 1970s. In 1980 she launched her "Pirate" look, which became linked with the contemporary "New Romantic" movement in pop. Throughout the eighties Westwood continued to produce original and even anarchic collections, including the

"Witches" show of 1983 and the "Mini-Crinolines" of 1985.

Yamamoto, Yohji (b. 1943) Japanese designer who formed his own company in 1972, showing his first collection in Japan in 1976. Uncompromising and anti-traditional, Yamamoto achieved considerable attention with his loose, unstructured but cleverly cut and swathed black-and-white garments. In the late eighties, Yamamoto began to allow more color to appear in his collections.

Reading List

Few books have so far been published specifically on eighties fashion. Magazines and films are always excellent sources for further investigation.

Adult General Reference Sources

Calasibetta, Charlotte, *Essential Terms of Fashion: A Collection of Definitions* (Fairchild, 1985).

Calasibetta, Charlotte, *Fairchild's Dictionary of Fashion*, 2nd Edition (Fairchild, 1988).
Gold, Annalee, *90 Years of Fashion* (Fairchild, 1990).
O'Hara, Georgina, *The Encyclopedia of Fashion* (Harry N. Abrams, 1986).
Trahey, Jane (Ed.), *100 Years of the American Female From Harper's Bazaar* (Random House, 1967).

Young Adult Sources

Ruby, Jennifer, *The Nineteen Sixties & Nineteen Seventies*, 'Costume in Context' series (David & Charles, 1989).
Wilcox, R. Turner, *Five Centuries of American Costume* (Scribner's, 1963).

Acknowledgments

The Author and Publishers would like to thank the following for permission to reproduce illustrations: Allsport for pages 16, 17, 32 and 48; The Camera Press for page 57; Comme des Garçons for pages 15, 21 and 37; Hulton Picture Company for page 6; Magnum for page 25; Rex Features for pages 7(a), 8, 9, 10, 11, 12, 13, 18, 19, 23, 27, 30(a), 31(b), 33(c), 34(b), 36, 39(a), 40, 41, 43(b), 47(c), 49, 50(b), 51(a), 55(a), 56 and 59(c). The illustrations were researched by David Pratt.

Time Chart

NEWS	EVENTS	FASHIONS
80 Iran-Iraq War breaks out New York transport strike Moscow Olympics Ronald Reagan elected US president	*The Face* begins publication Nightclubbing becomes new focus of youth culture "*Dallas*" reaches 300 million audience worldwide	Calvin Klein shirtwaists Ralph Lauren "frontier fashion" collection Vivienne Westwood Pirate look Karl Lagerfeld revives miniskirt
81 World economic recession US hostages released from Iran Martial law in Poland	Adam Ant "Stand and Deliver" video "New Romantic" movement	Knickerbockers in style Rei Kawakubo shows first collection in Paris Norma Kamali "sweats" collection
82 War in South Atlantic Israel invades Lebanon Warnings of danger from acid rain *Time* magazine names the computer "Man of the Year"	Prince has hit with "1999" Grandmaster Flash popularizes rap with "The Message"	Azzedine Alaia's first New York show Body Map label formed Armani shows culottes
83 Margaret Thatcher reelected as British prime minister	Breakdancing craze The term "yuppie" starts to gain wide currency	Gaultier slashed and layered look Boom in jogging suits and other exercise wear Kawakubo Paris show splits opinions
84 Walter Mondale runs for US president with Geraldine Ferraro but Reagan and Bush win the election Ethiopian famine	Band Aid Madonna emerges as a megastar Boom in dance movies	Donna Karan founds own label Gigli's "Italian Madonna" look
85 Mikhail Gorbachev becomes Soviet premier Anglo-Irish agreement on Northern Ireland	Live Aid AIDS recognized by World Health Organization as epidemic	St Laurent features short skirts, leather garments and cinched-in waists Neils Jorgensen, Daniel James and others show radical garments using rubber and Latex in original ways
86 *Challenger* space shuttle disaster Chernobyl nuclear disaster UK and France reach agreement to build Channel tunnel Irangate scandal in US	Fashion Aid	Christian Lacroix shows first couture collection
87 Glasnost takes off in USSR Margaret Thatcher elected for third term as British prime minister Stock market crash in October	Hugo Boss suits feature in "*LA Law*" "Yuppie" culture reaches its peak	Lycra gains wide popularity for leisure and party wear, no longer confined to exercise studio
88 End of the Cold War? Ceasefire in Gulf War George Bush elected US president Seoul Olympics	Acid House craze widely noted Flo-Jo makes big impact at Olympics	Aquagirl produces sporty look in Latex and other fabrics Retro looks for evening wear from Armani and others
89 Massive political change in Eastern Europe Berlin Wall breached Death of Ayatollah Khomeini Tiananmen Square massacre	*Batman* movie Barbara Bush as first lady promotes a stylish but matronly look for older women	Ripped jeans fad Yamamoto fifties Americana collection Fabrics come to the fore – paisley, lamé, African prints, lace, batiks

Fashion victim? Yet another extreme fashion statement – this time from Vivienne Westwood.

Index